W9-CEC-342

Team Spirit

THE NEW ORLEANS SAINTS

BY

MARK STEWART

Content Consultant
Jason Aikens
Collections Curator
The Professional Football Hall of Fame

NORWOOD HOUSE PRESS

CHICAGO, ILLINOIS

Norwood House Press
P.O. Box 316598
Chicago, Illinois 60631

For information regarding Norwood House Press, please visit our website at:
www.norwoodhousepress.com or call 866-565-2900.

PHOTO CREDITS:
All photos courtesy of AP Images—AP/Wide World Photos, Inc. except the following:
Topps, Inc. (6, 14, 20, 21 bottom, 22, 30, 34 bottom right, 36, 38,
40 top and bottom left & 43); Black Book Archives (9, 16, 17, 28,
35 top left and right & 41 top right); John Klein (21 top);
Author's Collection (34 bottom left & 40 bottom).
Special thanks to Topps, Inc.

Editor: Mike Kennedy
Associate Editor: Brian Fitzgerald
Designer: Ron Jaffe
Project Management: Black Book Partners, LLC.
Special thanks to: Margaret Graham and Terry Young

LIBRARY OF CONGRESS CATALOGING-IN-PUBLICATION DATA

Stewart, Mark, 1960-
   The New Orleans Saints / by Mark Stewart ; content consultant, Jason
Aikens.
      p. cm. -- (Team spirit)
   Summary: "Presents the history, accomplishments and key personalities of
the New Orleans Saints football team. Includes timelines, quotes, maps,
glossary and websites"--Provided by publisher.
   Includes bibliographical references and index.
   ISBN-13: 978-1-59953-132-8 (lib. bdg. : alk. paper)
   ISBN-10: 1-59953-132-1 (lib. bdg. : alk. paper)
   1. New Orleans Saints (Football team)--History--Juvenile literature. I.
Aikens, Jason. II. Title.
   GV956.N366S74 2008
   796.332'640976335--dc22
                                                          2007010098

COVER PHOTO: The Saints celebrate an exciting touchdown during the 2006 season.

Table of Contents

CHAPTER	PAGE
Meet the Saints	4
Way Back When	6
The Team Today	10
Home Turf	12
Dressed for Success	14
We Won!	16
Go-To Guys	20
On the Sidelines	24
One Great Day	26
Legend Has It	28
It Really Happened	30
Team Spirit	32
Timeline	34
Fun Facts	36
Talking Football	38
For the Record	40
Pinpoints	42
Play Ball	44
Glossary	46
Places to Go	47
Index	48

SPORTS WORDS & VOCABULARY WORDS: In this book, you will find many words that are new to you. You may also see familiar words used in new ways. The glossary on page 46 gives the meanings of football words, as well as "everyday" words that have special football meanings. These words appear in **bold type** throughout the book. The glossary on page 47 gives the meanings of vocabulary words that are not related to football. They appear in ***bold italic type*** throughout the book.

Meet the Saints

The people of New Orleans are fond of saying, "Let the good times roll." When life is fun, they try not to think about the things that disappoint them. They feel the same way about their football team, the Saints. If the Saints win, the good times keep rolling. If they lose, the fans try not to take it too hard.

The Saints are a team New Orleans loves to root for. Its players are daring, dashing, and sometimes even heroic. They fight hard—often against stronger opponents—and the fans cherish their victories. When you wear the black and gold, you are always part of the "good times."

This book tells the story of the Saints. During the team's first 39 years, football fans in New Orleans viewed Saints games as one of many fun things to do in America's favorite "party" town. In their 40th season, the Saints became a symbol of recovery and hope for a region crippled by a *natural disaster*.

Nate Lawrie watches as Joe Horn and Marques Colston celebrate a touchdown during a 2006 game. The Saints lifted people's spirits in New Orleans as the city recovered from Hurricane Katrina.

Way Back When

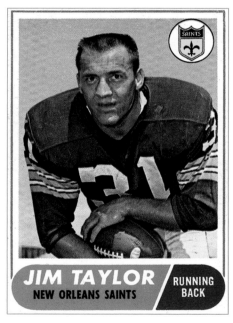

JIM TAYLOR
NEW ORLEANS SAINTS — RUNNING BACK

When the **National Football League (NFL)** decided to add new teams in the 1960s, one of the first cities it looked to was New Orleans, Louisiana. Football had long been a popular sport in the South, and NFL **exhibition games** held in New Orleans had always drawn big crowds. A group of *investors* headed by John Mecom Jr. was awarded a new team for the 1967 season. They called it the Saints, after one of the city's most famous songs, "When the Saints Go Marching In."

The team's first coach was Tom Fears, one of the greatest pass receivers in history. Fears built the Saints with experienced stars taken from other NFL teams. These players included Jim Taylor, Doug Atkins, Billy Kilmer, and Dave Whitsell. Over the next few seasons, the Saints found other good players, including kicker Tom Dempsey and receivers Danny Abramowicz and Dave Parks. Even so, every year the team lost more games than it won.

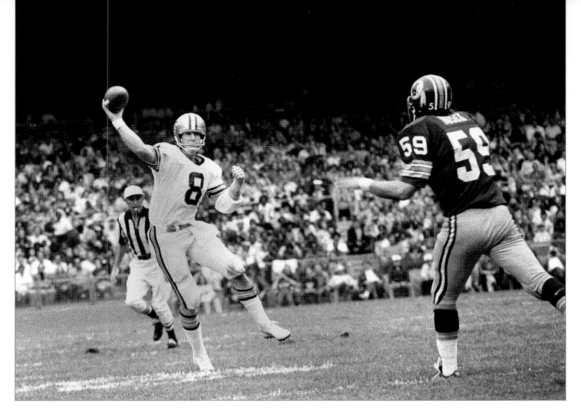

The first true star for the Saints was Archie Manning. In 1972, he finished tied for third in the NFL in touchdown passes, even though the Saints won just two games. Manning spent a lot of time running away from pass rushers during his time with the Saints. However, when he got the **blocking** he needed, he was one of the best quarterbacks in the league. Toward the end of the 1970s, the Saints looked like they would become a winning team. But in 1980, they lost their first 14 games before getting their one and only win of the year. Disappointed fans started calling them the "Aints."

LEFT: Jim Taylor, the team's leading rusher in its first season.
ABOVE: Archie Manning throws a pass on the run against the Washington Redskins.

Seven more years passed before New Orleans finally had its first winning season. The Saints were led by quarterback Bobby Hebert, running back Rueben Mayes, kicker Morten Andersen, and **kick returner** Mel Gray. The team had a great defense that starred linebackers Pat Swilling, Sam Mills, and Vaughan Johnson. Their coach, Jim Mora, pushed his players harder than anyone in the **National Football Conference (NFC)**. The extra work paid off. In 1987, the Saints went 12–3 and advanced to the **playoffs** for the first time.

The Saints continued to play well for many years. They put a number of talented stars on the field, including Eric Martin, Willie Roaf, Jim Everett, Eric Allen, Joe Johnson, and Craig "Ironhead" Heyward, one of the team's most popular players. The Saints advanced to the playoffs three years in a row—in 1990, 1991, and 1992. By the end of the *decade*, however, the team had sunk back to the bottom of the **NFC West**. The Saints began searching for a way to let the good times roll again.

LEFT: Bobby Hebert, who led the Saints to their first winning season.
ABOVE: Willie Roaf, the finest left tackle in the NFL during the 1990s.

The Team Today

The 21st century began with a bang for the Saints. They won the NFC West in 2000 and seemed to be building a good team in the years that followed. Exciting young players such as Charles Grant and Deuce McAllister gave fans something to cheer about.

Unfortunately, Hurricane Katrina hit New Orleans in August 2005 and threatened to change all of that. Like people all over the region, however, the Saints fought back. They got back on the right track in 2006.

The Saints *regrouped* with a new coach, a new attitude, and new players such as Drew Brees, Marques Colston, and Reggie Bush. Incredibly, they made it all the way to the **NFC Championship** game, coming within one victory of their first **Super Bowl.** Their heroic effort lifted the spirits of everyone in Louisiana—and set the stage for a new *era* of **professional** football in New Orleans.

Reggie Bush and Drew Brees, two of the newcomers who helped the Saints—and the city of New Orleans—bounce back from the disappointment of 2005.

Home Turf

The Saints played their first eight years in Tulane Stadium, the home field of Tulane University in New Orleans. Because of the hot and rainy weather in Louisiana, this outdoor stadium was only a temporary solution. The answer was to build an indoor arena. In 1975, the team moved into the brand new Louisiana Superdome. At the time, it was the largest domed structure in the world.

For many weeks after Hurricane Katrina, the Superdome was used as an emergency shelter. More than 20,000 people were stranded there when the city flooded. The dome's roof was also badly damaged. It took millions of dollars to *refurbish* the field so the Saints could move back in for the 2006 season.

BY THE NUMBERS

- *There are 69,703 seats for football games in the Superdome.*
- *As of 2006, the Saints had retired two numbers—31 (Jim Taylor) and 81 (Doug Atkins).*
- *Six Super Bowls were played in the Superdome between 1978 and 2002.*
- *The Superdome has been the home of the NCAA Basketball Tournament's "Final Four" four times.*

The lights shine brightly inside the Superdome before the Saints take the field for a workout.

Dressed for Success

The Saints have always featured the same colors in their uniforms—gold, black, and white. Before the team moved into the Superdome, they wore white jerseys at home in order to stay cool. Since then, they have preferred to wear dark jerseys for home games. The team does not worry about getting hot inside the dome, where air-conditioning keeps the temperature pleasant.

The Saints chose gold for the color of their helmets in 1967, their first season. During the preseason in 1969, the team tried black helmets. The Saints switched back to gold for the regular season and have kept this color ever since.

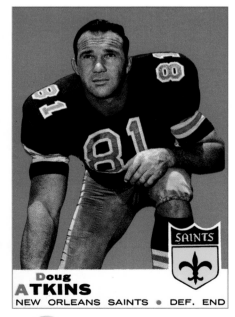

The team's **logo** is a *fleur-de-lis*, a flower-like symbol that has been used in France for more than 1,000 years. Louisiana was settled by the French in the 1700s, and the fleur-de-lis is a reminder of the state's past. The fleur-de-lis is a very popular symbol. It is also used by the Boy Scouts and Girl Scouts.

Doug Atkins models the Saints' first uniform. This trading card also shows the team's fleur-de-lis logo.

UNIFORM BASICS

The football uniform has three important parts—
- Helmet
- Jersey
- Pants

Helmets used to be made out of leather, and they did not have facemasks—ouch! Today, helmets are made of super-strong plastic. The uniform top, or jersey, is made of thick fabric. It fits snugly around a player so that tacklers cannot grab it and pull him down. The pants come down just over the knees.

There is a lot more to a football uniform than what you see on the outside. Air can be pumped inside the helmet to give it a snug, padded fit. The jersey covers shoulder pads, and sometimes a rib protector called a flak jacket. The pants include pads that protect the hips, thighs, *tailbone*, and knees.

Football teams have two sets of uniforms—one dark and one light. This makes it easier to tell two teams apart on the field. Almost all teams wear their dark uniforms at home and their light ones on the road.

The padding in Reggie Bush's uniform can be seen as he carries the ball down the field.

We Won!

During their first 40 seasons, the Saints fell short of their goal of reaching the Super Bowl. However, the fans will be talking about two of their playoff victories for a long, long time. The first came on December 30th, 2000. The Saints had just finished one of their best seasons. They won 10 games for new coach Jim Haslett and earned the NFC West title for just the second time.

The Saints' opponent in the opening round of the playoffs was the St. Louis Rams, who had won the Super Bowl the year before. Their offense was one of the most powerful in the league. The crowd that gathered at the Superdome was standing-room only, and the fans were on their feet for most of the game. The Rams scored first when Kurt Warner threw a touchdown pass to Isaac Bruce, but the Saints tightened their defense and did not allow another score until the fourth quarter.

By then, New Orleans had a 31–7 lead. The team's **rookie** quarterback, Aaron Brooks, had an amazing game. He picked the

St. Louis defense apart, firing one touchdown pass to Robert Wilson and three more to Willie Jackson. The fans, however, had to hold onto their seats as the Rams made a furious comeback. With the clock ticking down and the score 31–28, the Saints had to punt the ball to the Rams.

Everyone in the Superdome held their breath as the ball floated toward Az Hakim, the great St. Louis returner. Incredibly, Hakim muffed the punt and Brian Milne recovered the fumble to seal New Orleans' first-ever playoff victory.

On January 13th, 2007, the Saints moved one step closer to their dream of making the Super Bowl. They faced the Philadelphia Eagles in the playoffs, knowing that the winner would play for the NFC Championship. The game started well for New Orleans, as John Carney kicked two field goals for a 6–0 lead. At the beginning of the second quarter, however, the Eagles went ahead 7–6 on a long touchdown pass.

LEFT: Jim Haslett watches the Saints play in 2000.
ABOVE: Aaron Brooks, the rookie quarterback who led the Saints to their first playoff victory.

Drew Brees then took charge and led the Saints on a touchdown **drive**, with help from the team's two super rookies, Reggie Bush and Marques Colston. Once again, the Eagles responded with a score, and at halftime they led 14–13. The fans in the Superdome worried when Philadelphia began the third quarter with a touchdown to push the lead to 21–13. Could the Saints recover?

Thanks to Deuce McAllister, the answer was *yes*. He scored two touchdowns, while the defense held Philadelphia to a field goal. The final score was 27–24. The Saints had made it to their first NFC Championship game.

"This was an exciting win for this team, this organization, and this city," said coach Sean Payton after the game. "I couldn't be more proud of this group of guys that fought and battled all night."

LEFT: Deuce McAllister, whose two touchdowns helped beat the Eagles.
ABOVE: Coach Sean Payton and Jonathan Goodwin celebrate during the team's first trip to the NFC Championship game.

SAM MILLS Linebacker

SAM MILLS — Linebacker

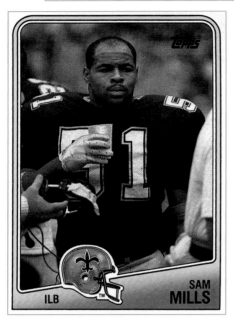

- BORN: 6/3/1959 • DIED: 4/18/2005
- PLAYED FOR TEAM: 1986 TO 1994

Sam Mills was one of the smallest linebackers in the NFL, but he was also one of the best. He was nicknamed the "Field Mouse" for the way he darted all over the field. Saints fans loved him because he never gave up on a play.

WILLIE ROAF   Offensive Lineman

- BORN: 4/18/1970
- PLAYED FOR TEAM: 1993 TO 2001

The Saints have had many good offensive **linemen**—including Jake Kupp, Stan Brock, and Brad Edelman—but none better than Willie Roaf. He went to the **Pro Bowl** six times with the Saints. With Roaf blocking, New Orleans runners and quarterbacks always knew they would be protected.

JOE HORN   Receiver

- BORN: 1/16/1972   • PLAYED FOR TEAM: 2000 TO 2006

Joe Horn worked as a dishwasher and in a factory before he decided to play pro football. After he joined the Saints, he became their top receiver and one of the best in the league. Horn tied for the NFC lead with 94 catches in 2004.

DEUCE McALLISTER   Running Back

- BORN: 12/27/1978 • FIRST SEASON WITH TEAM: 2001

The Saints **drafted** Deuce McAllister because he ran the ball with great determination. The big, powerful runner led the NFC in rushing in his first year as a starter. In 2006, he gained more than 1,000 yards for the fourth time in his career.

DREW BREES   Quarterback

- BORN: 1/15/1979 • FIRST SEASON WITH TEAM: 2006

The Saints needed a quarterback with a strong arm and great leadership skills. They took a chance on Drew Brees, who had hurt his right shoulder in 2005. The following year, he had the best season of any quarterback in the NFC.

REGGIE BUSH   Running Back

- BORN: 3/2/1985 • FIRST SEASON WITH TEAM: 2006

When the Saints drafted Reggie Bush, he *pledged* to help New Orleans rise from the destruction of Hurricane Katrina. The fans fell in love with the lightning-quick running back, who *dominated* opponents with his amazing speed and moves.

LEFT: Sam Mills
TOP RIGHT: Drew Brees
BOTTOM RIGHT: Reggie Bush

23

On the Sidelines

The Saints have had some of the NFL's most memorable coaches. Their first, Tom Fears, was elected to the **Hall of Fame** while with the team. After his coaching days were over, Fears became a special adviser on Hollywood football movies. The Saints' most *colorful* coach was Bum Phillips. He loved to joke with fans and reporters and wore a big cowboy hat wherever he went—except inside the Superdome.

Jim Mora was known for saying whatever was on his mind and for turning losing teams into winners. He was hired by Jim Finks, the team's boss off the field from 1986 to 1992. Mora was the first coach to guide the Saints to a winning record. Mike Ditka was also a bold and brash coach. He once traded all of the team's draft choices for running back Ricky Williams.

In 2006, Sean Payton became the Saints' coach. Payton believed that a great team needed great people. He looked for players who did well on the field and got along in the locker room. In 2006, Payton led the Saints to their first NFC Championship game.

Touchdown! Sean Payton celebrates a New Orleans score in 2006. The team went from 3–13 to 10–6 in his first season.

One Great Day

The 2005 season was a heartbreaking one for the Saints and their fans. The city of New Orleans had been badly damaged by Hurricane Katrina. Many residents died in the flooding, and thousands more were left homeless. The Saints were "homeless," too. They had to play their home games in other cities and won just three times.

The Saints returned to New Orleans in 2006. They hoped to lift the spirits of the city. Newcomers Drew Brees, Reggie Bush, and Marques Colston energized the team. Head coach Sean Payton, in his first season, filled his locker room with "good guys." The Saints won their first two games, which were played on the road. Their first home game came in the season's third week, against their biggest rivals—the Atlanta Falcons. It was televised across the nation on *Monday Night Football*.

That night, the Saints showed America that they were a very special team. On the first **series** of the game, Steve Gleason hurled his body through the air and blocked a punt by the Falcons. Teammate Curtis Deloatch pounced on the ball for a New Orleans touchdown. Later in the first half, Josh Bullocks broke through the Atlanta line to block a field goal.

Meanwhile, Brees led the Saints to one touchdown and three field goals. The Saints scored once on a tricky **double-reverse**. Bush and teammate Deuce McAllister piled up more than 100 yards against Atlanta, which was known for its good defense.

The New Orleans defense was sensational, too. Warrick Dunn, one of the NFL's top rushers, was stopped cold. Michael Vick, the Falcons' quarterback, was sacked five times. The final score was 23–3.

As the last few minutes melted away, thousands of people in the Superdome had tears streaming down their faces. The Saints and their fans had always shared a special closeness, but this victory brought them closer together than ever before.

LEFT: Marques Colston dodges tacklers against the Falcons.
ABOVE: Ernie Conwell hugs Mark Karney, who cannot hold back the tears after the Saints' victory.

27

It Really Happened

The 1970 season was one the Saints would rather forget. They won just twice that year. However, one of those victories will be remembered forever. On November 8th, the Saints played the Detroit Lions in Tulane Stadium. It was a tough battle. As usual, it looked as if New Orleans would come up short.

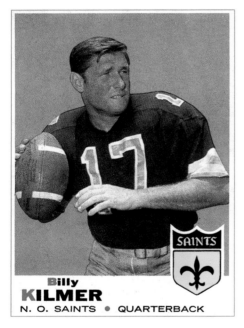

Billy
KILMER
N. O. SAINTS • QUARTERBACK

The Saints trailed 17–16 late in the fourth quarter. They had the ball on their own 28 yard line with only seconds left in the game. Billy Kilmer threw a 17-yard pass to Al Dodd, who stepped out of bounds to stop the clock. The Saints had time for one last play. Everyone in the stadium thought Kilmer would try a long pass into the end zone. They were shocked when they saw Tom Dempsey trot onto the field.

Dempsey was the team's kicker. He wore a special shoe on his right foot that helped him kick the ball. The Saints lined up with their **holder** on the 37 yard line. The goal posts were on the goal

line in those days, so Dempsey was looking at a 63-yard kick. The NFL record was 56 yards, which had stood unbroken for 17 years.

Jackie Burkett snapped the football, Joe Scarpati held it, and Dempsey kicked it as hard as he could. The ball cleared the **crossbar** by a few inches, and the Saints won 19–17. The celebration on the field and in the stands spilled out into the street, and soon the entire city was having a party.

"If you're going to set a record," Dempsey said, "this is the town to set it in. New Orleans people really know how to celebrate something!"

LEFT: Billy Kilmer, whose 17-yard pass gave Tom Dempsey a chance to kick his record field goal.   **ABOVE**: Dempsey swings his powerful right leg into the football in the final seconds against the Lions.

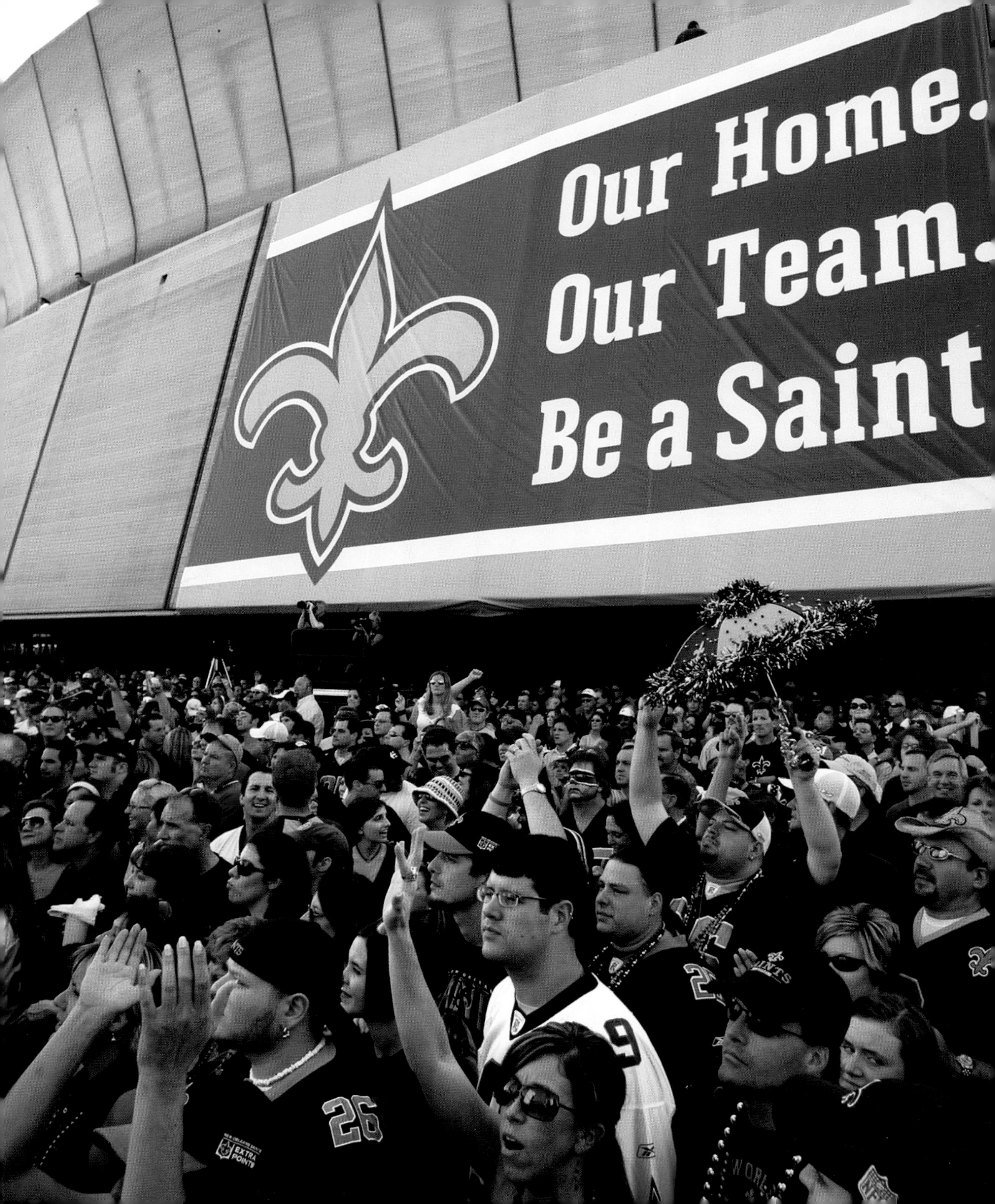
Our Home.
Our Team.
Be a Saint

Team Spirit

The Saints and their fans have had an unusually close bond since the team's start. In fact, more than 20,000 fans bought **season tickets** in the first few hours they went on sale in 1967. In the days before the Superdome opened, it was not unusual for 70,000 people to sit through a driving rainstorm to watch the team play.

When the Saints lost their first 14 games in 1980, it was embarrassing to root for them. Still, the fans supported the team, though some wore paper bags over their heads (with two eyeholes cut out) so no one would recognize them. It was their funny way of letting the team know it needed to improve—and fast!

In 2006, the fans welcomed the Saints back to the Superdome by buying every ticket available. The team thanked them with an emotional video tribute. Many fans wore paper bags to the games that season, but this time with holes cut big enough so that everyone could see their faces.

Fans gather in front of the Louisiana Superdome prior to its reopening in 2006. The Saints beat the Atlanta Falcons later that evening.

Timeline

In this timeline, the NFC Championship is listed under the year it was played. Remember that the NFC Championship and the Super Bowl are held early in the year and are actually part of the previous season. For example, Super Bowl XLI was played on February 4th, 2007, but it was the championship of the 2006 season.

1967
The Saints finish their first season at 3–11.

1981
George Rogers leads the NFL in rushing.

1969
Danny Abramowicz leads the NFL with 73 catches.

1972
Archie Manning leads the NFC in passing yards.

1979
Chuck Muncie becomes the team's first 1,000-yard rusher.

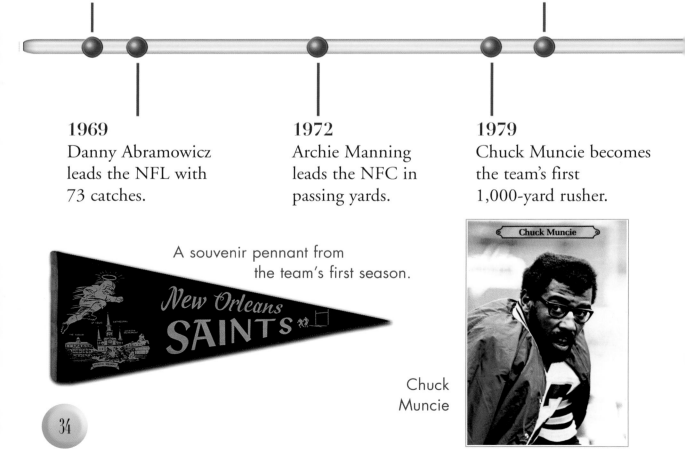

A souvenir pennant from the team's first season.

New Orleans SAINTS

Chuck Muncie

Chuck Muncie

Eric Allen, a Pro Bowl player in the 1990s.

Deuce McAllister

1991
New Orleans wins the NFC West for the first time.

2002
Deuce McAllister leads the NFC in rushing with 1,388 yards.

2000
The Saints win their first playoff game.

2006
Reggie Bush sets a record for rookie running backs with 88 catches.

2007
The Saints reach the NFC Championship game for the first time.

Reggie Bush

Fun Facts

SON SPOTS

Archie Manning was not the first Saint to have a son play quarterback in the NFL. Craig Kupp, who played for the Arizona Cardinals in 1991, was the son of Jake Kupp, New Orleans' first great offensive lineman.

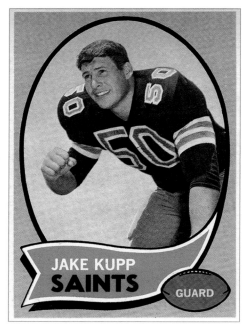

JAKE KUPP
SAINTS
GUARD

HIGH NOTE

In the Saints' first season, trumpeter Al Hirt played "When the Saints Go Marching In" after each New Orleans touchdown. Hirt owned a small part of the team.

DO IT AGAIN, DADDY!

On the first play in the team's history, John Gilliam returned a kickoff for a touchdown against the Los Angeles Rams. His wife and daughter missed the play because they were making a restroom visit!

ABOVE: Jake Kupp   **RIGHT**: The Bears cannot catch Reggie Bush as he streaks toward the end zone.

FIRST AND FOREMOST

The Saints' first Pro Bowl player was Dave Whitsell. He tied for the NFL lead with 10 **interceptions** in 1967.

FEARSOME FOURSOME

During the 1980s, Saints linebackers Vaughan Johnson, Pat Swilling, Sam Mills, and Rickey Jackson were known as the "Dome Patrol."

COOL BREES

In the 2006 NFC Championship game against the Chicago Bears, Drew Brees threw an 88-yard touchdown pass to Reggie Bush. It set a record for the longest play in a conference title game.

LEARNING CURVE

Kicker Morten Andersen had never seen a football until he came to the United States from Denmark in 1977 as a *foreign exchange* student. He ended up as the Saints' top all-time scorer.

Talking Football

SAINTS

ARCHIE MANNING • QB

"We were the only pro team in town. We weren't too good, but the fans were passionate about the Saints and extremely good to me and my family."
—*Archie Manning, on the city of New Orleans*

"You had to adjust to everything and then, all of a sudden, kick it into football gear. And that's hard. Trust me."
—*Joe Horn, on trying to get ready for football after Hurricane Katrina*

"We were as close a group of people as I have ever seen. I never felt that closeness ever again."
—*Pat Swilling, on the Saints of the early 1990s*

"I want to be out there running the ball, making plays, and scoring touchdowns. But at the same time, I've got to be patient and let it come to me."
—*Reggie Bush, on being a young player in the NFL*

ABOVE: Archie Manning   **RIGHT**: Drew Brees

"Success isn't permanent and failure isn't fatal."

—*Mike Ditka, on winning and losing*

"Getting drafted gave me an opportunity. That's all anyone can ever ask for. I was just able to take advantage of it."

—*Marques Colston, on how he went from unknown rookie to Saints star*

"There is still work to be done … the challenge is in front of us here."

—*Sean Payton, on the future of the Saints*

"We have a special bond with our fans and the people in this city."

—*Drew Brees, on what the Saints mean to New Orleans*

For the Record

T he great Saints teams and players have left their marks on the record books. These are the "best of the best" …

Pat Swilling

Rueben Mayes

SAINTS AWARD WINNERS

WINNER	AWARD	YEAR
Chuck Muncie	Pro Bowl **Most Valuable Player**	1980
George Rogers	NFL Offensive Rookie of the Year	1981
Rueben Mayes	NFL Offensive Rookie of the Year	1986
Jim Mora	NFL Coach of the Year	1987
Pat Swilling	NFL Defensive Player of the Year	1991
Joe Johnson	NFL Comeback Player of the Year	2000
Jim Haslett	NFL Coach of the Year	2000
Sean Payton	NFL Coach of the Year	2006

A pennant celebrating the Saints' 2006 division title.

SAINTS ACHIEVEMENTS

ACHIEVEMENT	YEAR
NFC Wild Card	1987
NFC Wild Card	1990
NFC West Champions	1991
NFC Wild Card	1992
NFC West Champions	2000
NFC South Champions	2006

Joe Johnson

Jeff Faine and Drew Brees hug Marques Colston after a touchdown during the Saints' amazing 2006 season.

Pinpoints

The history of a football team is made up of many smaller stories. These stories take place all over the map—not just in the city a team calls "home." Match the pushpins on these maps to the Team Facts and you will begin to see the story of the Saints unfold!

TEAM FACTS

1 New Orleans, Louisiana—*The Saints have played here since 1967.*

2 New Haven, Connecticut—*Joe Horn was born here.*

3 Neptune, New Jersey—*Sam Mills was born here.*

4 Steubenville, Ohio—*Danny Abramowicz was born here.*

5 Morehead City, North Carolina—*Vaughan Johnson was born here.*

6 Humboldt, Tennessee—*Doug Atkins was born here.*

7 Cleveland, Mississippi—*Archie Manning was born here.*

8 Glendale, California—*Jim Mora was born here.*

9 Portland, Oregon—*Stan Brock was born here.*

10 North Battleford, Saskatchewan, Canada—*Rueben Mayes was born here.*

11 Copenhagen, Denmark—*Morten Andersen was born here.*

12 Guadalajara, Mexico—*Tom Fears was born here.*

ARCHIE MANNING

QUARTERBACK
SAINTS

Archie Manning

Play Ball

Football is a sport played by two teams on a field that is 100 yards long. The game is divided into four 15-minute quarters. Each team must have 11 players on the field at all times. The group that has the ball is called the offense. The group trying to keep the offense from moving the ball forward is called the defense.

A football game is made up of a series of "plays." Each play starts and ends with a referee's signal. A play begins when the center snaps the ball between his legs to the quarterback. The quarterback then gives the ball to a teammate, throws (or "passes") the ball to a teammate, or runs with the ball himself. The job of the defense is to tackle the player with the ball or stop the quarterback's pass. A play ends when the ball (or player holding the ball) is "down." The offense must move the ball forward at least 10 yards every four downs. If it fails to do so, the other team is given the ball. If the offense has not made 10 yards after three downs—and does not want to risk losing the ball—it can kick (or "punt") the ball to make the other team start from its own end of the field.

At each end of a football field is a goal line, which divides the field from the end zone. A team must run or pass the ball over the goal line to score a touchdown, which counts for six points. After scoring a touchdown, a team can try a short kick for one "extra point," or try again to run or pass across the goal line for two points. Teams can score three points from anywhere on the field by kicking the ball between the goal posts. This is called a field goal.

The defense can score two points if it tackles a player while he is in his own end zone. This is called a safety. The defense can also score points by taking the ball away from the offense and crossing the opposite goal line for a touchdown. The team with the most points after 60 minutes is the winner.

Football may seem like a very hard game to understand, but the more you play and watch football, the more "little things" you are likely to notice. The next time you are at a game, look for these plays:

PLAY LIST

BLITZ—A play where the defense sends extra tacklers after the quarterback. If the quarterback sees a blitz coming, he passes the ball quickly. If he does not, he can end up at the bottom of a very big pile!

DRAW—A play where the offense pretends it will pass the ball, and then gives it to a running back. If the offense can "draw" the defense to the quarterback and his receivers, the running back should have lots of room to run.

FLY PATTERN—A play where a team's fastest receiver is told to "fly" past the defensive backs for a long pass. Many long touchdowns are scored on this play.

SQUIB KICK—A play where the ball is kicked a short distance on purpose. A squib kick is used when the team kicking off does not want the other team's fastest player to catch the ball and run with it.

SWEEP—A play where the ball carrier follows a group of teammates moving sideways to "sweep" the defense out of the way. A good sweep gives the runner a chance to gain a lot of yards before he is tackled or forced out of bounds.

Glossary

FOOTBALL WORDS TO KNOW

BLOCKING—Protection of the ball carrier by his teammates.

BROKEN PLAY—A play that does not go as planned.

CROSSBAR—The horizontal part of the goal post.

DOUBLE-REVERSE—A play using two handoffs to fool the defense.

DRAFTED—Chosen from a group of the best college players. The NFL draft is held each spring.

DRIVE—A series of plays by the offense that "drives" the defense back toward its own goal line.

EXHIBITION GAMES—Games that do not count towards a team's record, such as preseason games.

HALL OF FAME—The museum in Canton, Ohio where football's greatest players are honored. A player voted into the Hall of Fame is sometimes called a "Hall of Famer."

HOLDER—The player who keeps the ball steady for the kicker.

INTERCEPTIONS—Passes that are caught by the defensive team.

KICK RETURNER—A player selected by his team to catch kickoffs and punts and run them back.

LINEMEN—Players who begin each down crouched at the line of scrimmage.

MOST VALUABLE PLAYER (MVP)—The award given each year to the league's best player; also given to the best player in the Super Bowl and Pro Bowl.

NATIONAL FOOTBALL CONFERENCE (NFC)—One of two groups of teams that make up the National Football League. The winner of the NFC plays the winner of the American Football Conference (AFC) in the Super Bowl.

NATIONAL FOOTBALL LEAGUE (NFL)—The league that started in 1920 and is still operating today.

NFC CHAMPIONSHIP—The game played to determine which NFC team will go to the Super Bowl.

NFC WEST—A division for teams that play in the western part of the country.

PLAYOFFS—The games played after the season to determine which teams play in the Super Bowl.

PRO BOWL—The NFL's all-star game, played after the Super Bowl.

PROFESSIONAL—A player or team that plays a sport for money. College players are not paid, so they are considered "amateurs."

ROOKIE—A player in his first season.

ROUTES—The paths that receivers follow on pass plays.

SEASON TICKETS—Packages of tickets for each home game.

SERIES—A group of plays during which one team controls the ball.

SUPER BOWL—The championship of football, played between the winners of the NFC and AFC.

OTHER WORDS TO KNOW

COLORFUL—Lively and interesting.

DECADE—Period of 10 years; also a specific period, such as the 1950s.

DOMINATED—Completely controlled through the use of power.

ERA—A period of time in history.

FOREIGN EXCHANGE—An educational program that sends American students abroad and brings overseas students to the United States.

INVESTORS—People who spend their money for the purpose of making more money.

LEGISLATURE—A government group responsible for passing new state laws.

LOGO—A symbol or design that represents a company or team.

NATURAL DISASTER—An extreme event in nature such as a flood, hurricane, or earthquake that causes destruction and human suffering.

PLEDGED—Promised.

PRECISION—Accuracy or exactness.

REFURBISH—To make clean and fresh.

REGROUPED—Became organized in order to make a fresh start.

TAILBONE—The bone that protects the base of the spine.

Places to Go

ON THE ROAD

NEW ORLEANS SAINTS
1 Sugar Bowl Drive
New Orleans, Louisiana 70112
(504) 733-0255

THE PRO FOOTBALL HALL OF FAME
2121 George Halas Drive NW
Canton, Ohio 44708
(330) 456-8207

ON THE WEB

THE NATIONAL FOOTBALL LEAGUE www.nfl.com
  • *Learn more about the National Football League*

THE NEW ORLEANS SAINTS www.neworleanssaints.com
  • *Learn more about the New Orleans Saints*

THE PRO FOOTBALL HALL OF FAME www.profootballhof.com
  • *Learn more about football's greatest players*

ON THE BOOKSHELF

To learn more about the sport of football, look for these books at your library or bookstore:

  • Fleder, Rob–Editor. *The Football Book.* New York, NY: Sports Illustrated Books, 2005.
  • Kennedy, Mike. *Football.* Danbury, CT: Franklin Watts, 2003.
  • Savage, Jeff. *Play by Play Football.* Minneapolis, MN: Lerner Sports, 2004.

Index

PAGE NUMBERS IN **BOLD** REFER TO ILLUSTRATIONS.

Abramowicz, Danny 6, 20, **20**, 34, 43

Allen, Eric 9, **35**

Andersen, Morten 9, 21, **21**, 37, 43

Atkins, Doug 6, 13, **14**, 43

Brees, Drew **10**, 11, 19, 23, **23**, 26, 27, 37, 39, **39**, **41**

Brock, Stan 22, 43

Brooks, Aaron 16, **17**, 28, **28**

Bruce, Isaac 16

Bullocks, Josh 27

Burkett, Jackie 31

Bush, Reggie **10**, 11, **15**, 19, 23, **23**, 26, 27, 35, **35**, 37, **37**, 38

Carney, John 17

Colston, Marques **4**, 11, 19, 26, **26**, 39, **41**

Conwell, Ernie **27**

Deloatch, Curtis 27

Dempsey, Tom 6, 30, 31, **31**

Ditka, Mike 25, 39

Dodd, Al 30

Dunn, Warrick 27

Edelman, Brad 22

Everett, Jim 9

Faine, Jeff **41**

Fears, Tom 6, 25, 43

Finks, Jim 25

Geathers, Jumpy 29

Gilliam, John 36

Gleason, Steve 27

Goodwin, Jonathan **19**

Grant, Charles 11

Gray, Mel 9

Hakim, Az 17

Haslett, Jim 16, **16**, 40

Hebert, Bobby **8**, 9, 21, **21**

Heyward, Craig 9

Hirt, Al 36

Horn, Joe **4**, 22, 29, **29**, 38, 43

Jackson, Rickey 37

Jackson, Willie 17

Johnson, Joe 9, 40, **41**

Johnson, Vaughan 9, 37, 43

Karney, Mark **27**

Kilmer, Billy 6, 30, **30**

Kupp, Craig 36

Kupp, Jake 22, 36, **36**

Lawrie, Nate **4**

Lewis, Michael 28

Louisiana Superdome **12**, 13, 14, 16, 17, 19, 25, 27, 33

Manning, Archie 7, **7**, 20, 34, 36, 38, **38**, 43, **43**

Manning, Eli 20

Manning, Peyton 20

Martin, Eric 9

Mayes, Rueben 9, 40, **40**, 43

McAllister, Deuce 11, **18**, 19, 23, 27, 28, 35, **35**

Mecom, John Jr. 6

Mills, Sam 9, 22, **22**, 37, 43

Milne, Brian 17

Mora, Jim 9, 25, 40, 43

Muncie, Chuck 34, **34**, 40

Newton, Nate 29

Parks, Dave 6

Pathon, Jerome 28

Payton, Sean 19, **19**, **24**, 25, 26, 39, 40

Phillips, Bum 25

Roaf, Willie 9, **9**, 22

Rogers, George 34, 40

Scarpati, Joe 31

Stallworth, Donté 28

Swilling, Pat 9, 21, 37, 38, 40, **40**

Taylor, Jim 6, **6**, 13

Tulane Stadium 13, 30

Vick, Michael 27

Warner, Kurt 16

Whitsell, Dave 6, 37

Williams, Ricky 25

Wilson, Robert 17

The Team

MARK STEWART has written more than 20 books on football, and over 100 sports books for kids. He grew up in New York City during the 1960s rooting for the Giants and Jets, and now takes his two daughters, Mariah and Rachel, to watch them play in their home state of New Jersey. Mark comes from a family of

writers. His grandfather was Sunday Editor of *The New York Times* and his mother was Articles Editor of *The Ladies' Home Journal* and *McCall's*. Mark has profiled hundreds of athletes over the last 20 years. He has also written several books about New York and New Jersey. Mark is a graduate of Duke University, with a degree in History. He lives with his daughters and wife Sarah overlooking Sandy Hook, New Jersey.

JASON AIKENS is the Collections Curator at the Pro Football Hall of Fame. He is responsible for the preservation of the Pro Football Hall of Fame's collection of artifacts and memorabilia and obtaining new donations of memorabilia from current players and NFL teams. Jason has a Bachelor of Arts in History from Michigan State University and a Master's in History from Western Michigan University where he concentrated on sports history. Jason has been working for the Pro Football Hall of Fame since 1997;

before that he was an intern at the College Football Hall of Fame. Jason's family has roots in California and has been following the St. Louis Rams since their days in Los Angeles, California. He lives with his wife Cynthia and recent addition to the team Angelina in Canton, Ohio.